TRUE LEADERS
WITH
HEART

TRUE LEADERS
WITH
HEART

WEEKLY MEDITATIONS FOR LEADERS

KARLA NIVENS

XULON PRESS

Xulon Press
2301 Lucien Way #415
Maitland, FL 32751
407.339.4217
www.xulonpress.com

Printed in the United States of America.

ISBN-13: 978-1-5456-7847-3

ACKNOWLEDGEMENTS

I tell the story often of my six-year-old, short-legged self falling off the brick fireplace in our family room because I thought the fireplace was my stage. In my mind, when you see a stage, you get on it to worship the Lord. Every member of my family knew I would become a worship leader at the professional level. My husband, Dr. Roosevelt Nivens Jr., saw me as an inspirational leader. Roosevelt, I thank you for your vision of me and your vision for our family. You are my example of a True Leader with Heart. I continue to be in love with you!

To my children, Naomi & Roosevelt III — you are the reason I push myself to expand my territory. I am proud of my teenagers! I love you both!

To my parents and brothers and sisters-in-love — you are my guides. The Lord has placed creativity and ingenuity in our hearts. Let's continue to serve the body of Christ with excellence. I love you!

To my father-in-love and mother-in-love in heaven — you have already given me the best gift I could ask for in Dr. Roosevelt Nivens Jr., but you continue to bless me by showering me with your prayers. I love you!

To my Love Ministries family — thank you for your constant and unwavering support. You have always given me room to grow the gifts God has given me. I appreciate having you as a home base all through the years.

To my Highland Park family — I will never forget my first Sunday in Cornerstone almost fifteen years ago. I immediately felt at home and immediately felt comfortable entering into worship with you. Thank you for being my church family and for accepting the Nivens family into your hearts!

To the Cornerstone band — words cannot express my gratitude to you! You are my friends, my business partners, and my family all wrapped in one. I respect each of you and PRAY the Lord will allow us the opportunity to continue in worship together for many, many more years to come! You are my inspiration for the words written in these pages.

YOU ARE THE LEADER THE WORLD NEEDS

W hat is a leader? Do you see yourself fitting the definition of a leader? Would the people in your community categorize you as a leader?

> "Leadership is having the capacity to remove barriers and the ability to influence people to be their absolute best" – Dr. Roosevelt Nivens Jr.

> "If your actions inspire others to dream more, learn more, do more and become more, you are a leader." – John Quincy Adams

> *Pozin, I. (2014). 16 Leadership Quotes To Inspire You To Greatness [Article]. Retrieved from https://www. forbes.com/sites/ilyapozin/2014/04/10/16-leadership-quotes-to-inspire-you-to-greatness/#1c3be0a067ad*

Scripture leads us into viewing ourselves as leaders:

> **God:** [26] Now let Us conceive *a new creation—* humanity—*made* in Our image, *fashioned* according to Our likeness. And let *Us grant* them authority over all the earth—the fish in the sea and the birds in the sky, the domesticated animals and the *small* creeping creatures on the earth. [27] So God did *just that*. He created humanity in His image, created

them male and female. ²⁸ Then God blessed them and gave them *this directive*: "Be fruitful and multiply. Populate the earth. *I make you trustees of My estate,* so care for My creation and rule over the fish of the sea, the birds of the sky, and every creature that roams across the earth."

Genesis 1: 26-28 (The Voice)

See yourself as a person who others depend on to help them succeed in life. Imagine yourself at your very best. The very best you can do in life is helping people in your community. This is leadership. You may be a high-powered CEO, you may be a teacher, you may be a parent, you may be a community activist, you may be a caretaker of a building – wherever you are in life, it's up to you to see yourself as a servant leader. True Leaders with Heart consider those in their care. True Leaders with Heart consider their words before they speak. True Leaders with Heart desire to lead with great integrity. Most importantly, True Leaders with Heart are devoted followers of Jesus Christ. Leader, find the inspiration you need to lead with heart within the pages of these weekly meditations. The Lord loves you and loves the individuals you lead. You have the Heart of a True Leader!

WEEK 1:

1 John 2:1-2 (MSG) — I write this, dear children, to guide you out of sin. But if anyone does sin, we have a Priest-Friend in the presence of the Father: Jesus Christ, righteous Jesus. When he served as a sacrifice for our sins, he solved the sin problem for good—not only ours, but the whole world's.

This scripture has great truth for leaders to wrestle with. We all have a sinful nature, but we shouldn't set out planning to live in sin. Our chief love shouldn't be an attitude of sin. However, we sometimes struggle trying to be free of sinful traps. We let ourselves down, and we often let others down. But leaders who have a heart to repent or say they are sorry for their sin and become determined to move forward are leaders who understand God's grace. These are people who have thriving relationships with Jesus. Jesus is and will always be a sufficient sacrifice for our sin. And even though we live in a world that makes a lot of excuses for sin and a world that gives us permission to do whatever we please, we must still choose to follow the Lord. We aren't perfect, and we will never, ever reach perfection. But as we worship the Lord on a weekly basis, we become leaders who realize we worship a God who is forgiving, loving, and gracious. He alone has solved our sin problem and has renamed us righteous leaders. It is our responsibility to stay in the mindset of people who repent daily and offer our lives to be used for His glory.

WEEK 2:

Isaiah 26:3-4 (MSG) — People with their minds set on you, you keep completely whole, Steady on their feet, because they keep at it and don't quit. Depend on God and keep at it because in the Lord God you have a sure thing.

L eaders must remember to meditate on the Word of God constantly. If you lose your composure easily, it will set the tone for your entire team to operate in chaos. Leaders are confident in their ability to problem solve and their ability to motivate their teams to problem solve because of one simple fact — their confidence is in the Lord. Tap into a supply of peace supplied by the Everlasting Rock. It is the Lord who has appointed you into a position of leadership, and it will be the Lord who remains your never-ending support. It seems our world is searching for peace — inward peace, outward peace, peace under pressure, peace as we pray and support those we lead. The only perfect peace that will never fail is found in the Lord. Remind yourself of how the Lord is aware of everything you're facing and remember to repeat Scripture throughout the day. We can have peace as we build our character by remaining mindful of our Savior, who is leading us through every single day of our lives. Our confidence is in Him.

WEEK 3:

Psalm 25:1-10 (NIV) — In you, Lord my God, I put my trust. I trust in you; do not let me be put to shame, nor let my enemies triumph over me. No one who hopes in you will ever be put to shame, but shame will come on those who are treacherous without cause. Show me your ways, Lord, teach me your paths. Guide me in your truth and teach me, for you are God my Savior, and my hope is in you all day long. Remember, Lord, your great mercy and love, for they are from of old. Do not remember the sins of my youth and my rebellious ways; according to your love remember me, for you, Lord, are good. Good and upright is the Lord; therefore he instructs sinners in his ways. He guides the humble in what is right and teaches them his way. All the ways of the Lord are loving and faithful toward those who keep the demands of his covenant.

Did you know our prayers never die? When you pray a prayer for yourself, for your children, for your family, for your job, or for our nation, the prayer stays before the Lord, and He, being a great Shepherd, is constantly covering our lives. The Lord is completely trustworthy. We can trust Him with the details of our lives. He wants the best for you, and He wants to get the best through you so the team you're leading gets the best leader possible. A prayer humbly spoken to the Lord accomplishes so much. Leader, pray for everything concerning the team you serve. Remain thankful for each individual and thankful for the circumstances which brought him or her to your team. Celebrate the uniqueness of their lives and personalities. Thank the Lord for the special way they view the world as well as how they approach the job you do every day. Diversity is always proof of how the Spirit of the Lord can unite a group of people to accomplish a goal. Great leaders see diversity as an asset and not a hindrance. After you spend time praying for your team, let each person know how proud you are of them and how thankful you are for their commitment to the work you do weekly. As you meditate on this scripture, ask the Holy Spirit to help you lead well. Humbly ask the Lord to bring glory to His name through all your team accomplishes.

WEEK 4:

Matthew 11:28-30 (MSG) — "Are you tired? Worn out? Burned out on religion? Come to me. Get away with me and you'll recover your life. I'll show you how to take a real rest. Walk with me and work with me—watch how I do it. Learn the unforced rhythms of grace. I won't lay anything heavy or ill-fitting on you. Keep company with me and you'll learn to live freely and lightly."

The ways to knowledge, wisdom, rest for your soul, and true satisfaction in life are found in the Lord. Nothing replaces quiet time, reading Scripture, praying, or personal worship time. It's impossible to be at your best without slowing down to meditate on the Word of God. His words lead us into finding peace so we can rest in the love of God and lead others well. Many times, leaders are taught to be good listeners, good communicators, always positive, and always ready for change, but before you can be any of these things, leaders must spend time with the Lord. Seek the Lord first and keep Him first. When we all get heaven, we will have perfect rest, and we will worship Him with complete joy. But, why wait for heaven? Bring heaven to earth now! Be a humble leader who seeks the Lord and be influential in getting those you lead to do the same.

WEEK 5:

2 Corinthians 5:19-21 (MSG) — God put the world square with himself through the Messiah, giving the world a fresh start by offering forgiveness of sins. God has given us the task of telling everyone what he is doing. We're Christ's representatives. God uses us to persuade men and women to drop their differences and enter into God's work of making things right between them. We're speaking for Christ himself now: Become friends with God; he's already a friend with you. How? you ask. In Christ. God put the wrong on him who never did anything wrong, so we could be put right with God.

As believers of Jesus Christ, we have received grace. We cannot earn grace or ever deserve Christ's sacrificing His life. You may have learned John 3:16 as a child in Sunday school. John 3:16 says that God loved the world so much that He gave His "only" Son as a sacrifice for our sin. Whoever believes in Him is saved. We are saved and are now called to a higher purpose in Christ. We've received righteousness from our loving Savior. It is our job to connect with as many people as we can and to be a mediator between them and the Lord. We want to bring people close to Christ so they can receive from Him the same grace we've received. Your leadership should make people wonder where your joyful spirit draws its strength from. Take some time to meditate on the scripture above and be thankful for God's calling on your life. Since God has placed you in a leadership role, let your life be extremely persuasive in bringing a message of hope to everyone around you.

WEEK 6:

1 Timothy 6:17-19 (MSG) — Tell those rich in this world's wealth to quit being so full of themselves and so obsessed with money, which is here today and gone tomorrow. Tell them to go after God, who piles on all the riches we could ever manage—to do good, to be rich in helping others, to be extravagantly generous. If they do that, they'll build a treasury that will last, gaining life that is truly life.

Sometimes life has many uncertain things which seem to happen. The economy goes up and down, or there's a natural disaster; your family faces a serious illness or a death in the family, or you face difficulties at work and home. Many things are out of your control, and riches aren't promised, nor are they necessary for living a great life. This scripture encourages you to enjoy life. Enjoying life means living not only for yourself but for others — serving your family, helping those in need, and telling others about the love you've found in the Lord. In every season of your life, Leader, you live an extremely blessed life, and you are doing exactly what we were born to do. You are rich in the areas where it counts, for sure. Enjoy the process you go through to prepare to lead your team. Care for them, pray for them and with them, and work as a healthy team toward your goals. Your team will take its cue from you — the expressions on your face, your character, the tone you use when communicating. Is your leadership sending the message that you love, adore, and worship a great and holy God? Honor Him with the gift of leadership He has given you. That is the definition of enjoying a rich life.

WEEK 7:

Romans 12:1-2 (MSG) — So here's what I want you to do, God helping you: Take your everyday, ordinary life—your sleeping, eating, going-to-work, and walking-around life—and place it before God as an offering. Embracing what God does for you is the best thing you can do for him. Don't become so well-adjusted to your culture that you fit into it without even thinking. Instead, fix your attention on God. You'll be changed from the inside out. Readily recognize what he wants from you, and quickly respond to it. Unlike the culture around you, always dragging you down to its level of immaturity, God brings the best out of you, develops well-formed maturity in you.

Have you ever decided to all of a sudden make bold decisions about your life? You could decide to hold yourself accountable for praying every day without fail or decide to say something nice to a random person once a day. Everyone has the freedom to change their habits so people can see more of God in them. After all, how will a world full of people who are searching for a better way find the Lord if they don't see Him through our actions? People rarely all of a sudden open the Bible one day. Normally, they get introduced to the Lord through other people. The Lord's will for your life is for people to find love, grace, and acceptance through you. Make a bold decision today to improve an area of your leadership. You may need to share your decision with someone you trust and ask them to check in with you to see if you are sticking with the change. If you mess up and return to old habits, put it behind you and get back on track. Be a bold leader who is not afraid to make the necessary changes to become more like Jesus.

WEEK 8:

Psalm 100 (MSG) —A thanksgiving Psalm
On your feet now—applaud GOD! Bring a gift of
laughter, sing yourselves into his presence. Know
this: GOD IS GOD, AND GOD, GOD. He made us; we
didn't make him. We're his people, his well-tended
sheep. Enter with the password: "Thank you!"
Make yourselves at home, talking praise. Thank
him. Worship him. For GOD IS SHEER BEAUTY, all-gen-
erous in love, loyal always and ever.

Do you ever have to talk yourself into going to work? Many leaders have to give themselves a pep talk before the commute to work. Or maybe someone on your team is dealing with a personal issue that seems to somehow affect the culture negatively. What's the best thing to do when your work life isn't easy? Psalm 100 gives leaders and everyone a charge — worship! God has promised to be with us, but we will go through difficult times. Worship through your difficulties and thank God for the people on your team. Keep praying for them no matter what. Continue to share the love of God with everyone. Ask the Lord for inventive ways to influence the culture. The Lord will be faithful to you; you just need to remain faithful to Him.

WEEK 9:

Psalm 66:8-12 (MSG) — Bless our God, O peoples! Give him a thunderous welcome! Didn't he set us on the road to life? Didn't he keep us out of the ditch? He trained us first, passed us like silver through refining fires, brought us into hardscrabble country, pushed us to our very limit, road-tested us inside and out, took us to hell and back; Finally he brought us to this well-watered place.

This scripture paints the picture of real life. Joyfully and exuberantly praise the Lord for being your Shepherd because you can think of many times when the favor of the Lord has kept you. God loves us enough to teach us how to live in a way that brings Him glory. Great parents teach, guide, discipline, and help shape their children's character, and that's exactly what the Lord does for us. Sometimes, we go through circumstances designed to bring out the very best in us, and when we look back through all we've made it through, we recognize how strong we've become because of the grace of God. Allow the knowledge of His mighty hand to motivate you to honor Him. He is so deserving of your adoration! Now, it is your duty to do the same for those you lead. Help people work their way through issues, mold them into leaders by encouraging them with your words, and show them an example of godly character by the way you lead.

WEEK 10:

Luke 1:46-50 (NIV) — Mary's Song
And Mary said: "My soul glorifies the Lord and my
spirit rejoices in God my Savior, for he has been
mindful of the humble state of his servant. From
now on all generations will call me blessed, for the
Mighty One has done great things for me—holy is
his name. His mercy extends to those who fear him,
from generation to generation.

This scripture is the song Mary's heart sang as she was chosen to be the mother of Jesus. This is scripture leaders should use as a meditation guide. Mary was overwhelmed with reverence for the Lord. She recognized that God is good and should be glorified. He has an extraordinary plan for our lives, and His plan for us is special, unique, and grand. All of us can sit down and write down so many blessings we've been given. It's important for us to actively remember our blessings so we don't become ungrateful, cynical leaders. Cynicism creates a very toxic work environment. To combat sinking into a cycle of cynicism, actually look back over the years and see the Lord's hand of protection on your life. Follow Mary's example — magnify the Lord and rejoice in your Savior with great joy!

WEEK 11:

1 Corinthians 13:3-7 (MSG) — If I give everything I own to the poor and even go to the stake to be burned as a martyr, but I don't love, I've gotten nowhere. So, no matter what I say, what I believe, and what I do, I'm bankrupt without love. Love never gives up. Love cares more for others than for self. Love doesn't want what it doesn't have. Love doesn't strut, Doesn't have a swelled head, Doesn't force itself on others, Isn't always "me first," Doesn't fly off the handle, Doesn't keep score of the sins of others, Doesn't revel when others grovel, Takes pleasure in the flowering of truth, Puts up with anything, Trusts God always, Always looks for the best, Never looks back, But keeps going to the end.

The motivation behind your leadership should be love. Forgiveness, grace, benevolence, and yes–leading people well are all motivated by love. Leader, do you practice looking at those you lead with great compassion? The Lord does. Even when we've had a bad week, or we've been wronged by someone, or we're feeling tired, or we've made bad decisions; the Lord still looks at all of His children with great compassion. Take time to prepare yourself for your week by praying about issues in your personal life. Ask the Lord for healing and a word of peace you can remember throughout the week. Preparation is critical for leaders. If you don't have time for personal worship, prayer, and meditation on the truth of God's word, you will not be a leader motivated by God's love.

WEEK 12:

Psalm 66:1-6 (MSG) — All together now—applause for God! Sing songs to the tune of his glory, set glory to the rhythms of his praise. Say of God, "We've never seen anything like him!" When your enemies see you in action, they slink off like scolded dogs. The whole earth falls to its knees— it worships you, sings to you, can't stop enjoying your name and fame. Take a good look at God's wonders— they'll take your breath away. He converted sea to dry land; travelers crossed the river on foot. Now isn't that cause for a song?

The psalmist is leading you to praise God, to glorify Him, to recognize His worth, and to remember how good the Lord is. The psalmist also leads you to think of specific things God has done for you. How has God shown His wisdom, power, and faithfulness to you? Life goes on day after day, and you may forget to give God credit for the little things He's done for you. Leaders can attribute too many things to hard work, sound decision-making skills, and fine leadership abilities. But since you have made the choice to accept the Lord as your Savior, you should recognize the wisdom He's given you. He has allowed you to hone your skills so you can have a part in leading His people. Approach this week with a fresh perspective. Take some time to remember how you have seen the Lord work in your life and in your ability to motivate and lead others. Thank the Lord for His handiwork in your life while you exhibit leadership motivated by the love of Jesus Christ.

WEEK 13:

Isaiah 43:1-3 (MSG) — But now, God's Message, the God who made you in the first place, Jacob, the One who got you started, Israel: "Don't be afraid, I've redeemed you. I've called your name. You're mine. When you're in over your head, I'll be there with you. When you're in rough waters, you will not go down. When you're between a rock and a hard place, it won't be a dead end— Because I am God, your personal God, The Holy of Israel, your Savior.

Leader, think back through your career path. Have you ever encountered a boss who said to you, "Don't be afraid; I've got you. You belong to me. When you go through rough waters, I'll save you. If you happen to make a mistake, I'll redeem your mistake as if it was my own mistake." How hard would people work if they knew their leadership had their backs? News flash — this is how the Lord leads us. We learn how to receive comfort from the Lord by going through tough times together. God doesn't promise His children a life of ease. He promises to provide us with what we need to keep moving forward. We can firmly say we have experienced God as Savior, as Peace, as Comfort, as Healer, as Friend, as the One who delivers, and as Lord. Consider going deeper in your faith with the Lord and in your dependence on Him. He is your source yesterday, today, and always. He has carefully placed you in a position of leadership, and He wants you, plus everyone with you, to prosper. He wants your leadership skills to be so sharp that your business has success plus people get closer to Christ because of how you live. That's what the Lord will do through you as you depend on Him every single day. May God receive all glory, honor, and praise!

WEEK 14:

2 Corinthians 5:14-20 (The Voice) — You see, the controlling force in our lives is the love of the Anointed One. And our confession is this: One died for all; therefore, all have died. He died for us so that we will all live, not for ourselves, but for Him who died and rose from the dead. Because of all that God has done, we now have a new perspective. We used to show regard for people based on worldly standards and interests. No longer. We used to think of the Anointed the same way. No longer. Therefore, if anyone is united with the Anointed One, that person is a new creation. The old life is gone— and see—a new life has begun! All of this is a gift from our Creator God, who has pursued us and brought us into a restored and healthy relationship with Him through the Anointed. And He has given us the same mission, the ministry of reconciliation, to bring others back to Him. It is central to our good news that God was in the Anointed making things right between Himself and the world. This means He does not hold their sins against them. But it also means He charges us to proclaim the message that heals and restores our broken relationships with God and each other. So we are now representatives of the Anointed One, the Liberating King; God has given us a charge to carry through our lives—urging all people on behalf of the Anointed to become reconciled to the Creator God. He orchestrated this: the Anointed One, who had never experienced sin, became sin for us so that in Him we might embody the very righteousness of God.

This passage has so many nuggets for leaders. A transformation happened through the work of the Holy Spirit, and it has renewed your life in a way that's so powerful! You aren't a regular, run-of-the-mill person. You have power from God to change the world. You will have challenges and rough times, but the Holy Spirit will lead you through them every day. You can no longer live just for yourself; you live for the glory of God. You lead people for the glory of God. You lead people into the knowledge of God as Savior. If the people on your team are used to you second-guessing every decision they make and you haven't shown them how to make decisions on their own, then today is a good day for change. Build people up, show them how to lead, and give them the structure to create a winning team. Leadership doesn't mean a slave owner or a person who has direct reports. Travis Bradberry wrote this definition of "leadership" for Entrepreneur Magazine: "Leadership is a process of social influence which maximizes the efforts of others toward the achievement of a greater good. Influencing others is the key to a successful working environment and a successful life."

Bradberry, T. (2015). What Really Makes a Good Leader? [Article]. Retrieved from https://www. entrepreneur.com/article/249905

WEEK 15:

Philippians 1:6, 9-11 (The Voice) — I am confident that the Creator, who has begun such a great work among you, will not stop in mid-design but will keep perfecting you until the day Jesus the Anointed, our Liberating King, returns to redeem the world.

Here's what I pray for you: Father, may their love grow more and more in wisdom and insight— so they will be able to examine and determine the best from everything else. And on the day of the Anointed One, the day of His judgment, let them stand pure and blameless, filled with the fruit of righteousness that ripens through Jesus the Anointed.

Paul and Timothy wrote these words to the church in Philippi. Try reading this scripture every day for a week. God has something special and unique planned for your life that will impact the kingdom of God. Not only does He have plans, but you can personally count on Him to not give up on you until you accomplish what your life was set to accomplish. When God begins something in us, He will finish it, and He will supply what we need to accomplish the good work He has set for us to do. Why has God called you into leadership? It's because you have the capacity to lead with grace because you know the love of the Lord. You can confidently model Christ to everyone — that's kingdom leadership. Scripture tells us to guard ourselves from quitting early when doing good. Leading others takes daily commitment. Without a deep and personal relationship with the Lord, we can't go before people to lead them. Don't forget to spend daily time worshiping the Lord and meditating on Scripture to build yourself up in truth.

WEEK 16:

Hebrews 13:1-7 (The Voice) — Let love continue among you. Don't forget to extend your hospitality to all—even to strangers—for as you know, some have unknowingly shown kindness to heavenly messengers in this way. Remember those imprisoned for their beliefs as if you were their cellmate; and care for any who suffer harsh treatment, as you are all one body. Hold marriage in high esteem, all of you, and keep the marriage bed pure because God will judge those who commit sexual sins. Keep your lives free from the love of money, and be content with what you have because He has said, "I will never leave you; I will always be by your side." Because of this promise, we may boldly say, The Lord is my help— I won't be afraid of anything. How can anyone harm me? Listen to your leaders, who have spoken God's word to you. Notice the fruits of their lives and mirror their faith.

Have you ever taken the time to get to know and understand the people you lead? Notice their character and care about the state of their lives. Care about those who are broken-hearted and those who are sick, as well as those who are filled with great joy. What would happen if you set the tone for creating an office full of people who are concerned for each other? It doesn't matter what race people are, what political party they stand for, where they were born, where they currently live, or where they are in their career — everyone likes to feel as though someone truly cares about them. Everyone needs to hear how much God cares for them as well. We all need to hear the Lord speak His promise to always be with else every single day. We all need to know the Lord will never, ever walk away from us. Even when we fail and fall short, He has promised to take the detours in our lives and make them into something beautiful that can be used to glorify Him. Leader, always care about people and help people find the truth about Jesus Christ.

WEEK 17:

Psalm 119: 10-11 (The Voice) — I have pursued You with my whole heart; do not let me stray from Your commands. Deep within me I have hidden Your word so that I will never sin against You.

Psalm 119 focuses on living your life in praise to God while recognizing His grace that covers your life. One of the reasons people should want to work under your leadership is because you have demonstrated that you really love the Lord. You are genuine in all you do. Study examples of other successful leaders and consider how you can learn from their successes. Leader, while you are sharpening your professional skills, remember to sharpen your spiritual skills. Knowing scripture will also enable you to be a better leader. Pursue the Lord with the same passion as you pursue success in your career. Depend on His grace and connect your heart with the Lord's while studying scripture.

WEEK 18:

Zephaniah 3:14-17 (The Voice) — Hurray! It's time to sing, faithful daughter of Zion! It's time to shout out loud, Israel! Be happy and celebrate with all your being, faithful children of Jerusalem! The Eternal has cancelled His judgments against you. He changed the course of your enemies. The True King of Israel, the Eternal One, is standing right here among you; you have no reason to be afraid ever again. On that day people will say to the faithful in Jerusalem, "Do not be afraid, Zion; Hold your head and hands high, and take courage." The Eternal your God is standing right here among you, and He is the champion who will rescue you. He will joyfully celebrate over you; He will rest in His love for you; He will joyfully sing because of you like a new husband.

It seems so many leaders get caught in a cycle of grief, worry, and fear that cripples. Maggie is a young lady who grew up in poverty without her dad ever being present in her life. Her mom died after her first year in college, and then years later, her brother died on her birthday. Every birthday, Maggie's caught between a battle of celebrating her birthday or mourning the fact that her eight-year-old niece had to be the one to alert a neighbor about her dad lying unconscious in their kitchen. Terrible and unthinkable things sometimes happen in this life. Many times, joy is a decision. Leadership is obviously one of your major gifts and callings. You can operate in your God-given gifts to help Him demonstrate how much the Lord loves and cares for His people. He is forgiving your sins while delightfully giving you grace. He rejoices over those who faithfully serve Him. Leader, consider how you can care for anyone facing major challenges in their personal life.

WEEK 19:

1 Thessalonians 5:13-18 (MSG) — Get along among yourselves, each of you doing your part. Our counsel is that you warn the freeloaders to get a move on. Gently encourage the stragglers, and reach out for the exhausted, pulling them to their feet. Be patient with each person, attentive to individual needs. And be careful that when you get on each other's nerves you don't snap at each other. Look for the best in each other, and always do your best to bring it out. Be cheerful no matter what; pray all the time; thank God no matter what happens. This is the way God wants you who belong to Christ Jesus to live.

This scripture was written for those in leadership. This is how a team should function. When you are an individual who is one part of a whole team, it is your responsibility to be your brother's keeper. Team members should not think or speak negatively of anyone associated with their team — even when negativity may be warranted, work to stay positive. Help each other to improve because you are all vital parts of the team as a whole. Every individual is needed and valuable so the entire team can thrive and be successful. Successful team members give comfort when it's needed and show grace and love to each other even when it's not deserved. Leader, continue to follow the Lord in your personal life and encourage your team members to follow Him as a team.

WEEK 20:

John 14:16-17 (The Voice) — I will ask the Father to send you another Helper, the Spirit of truth, who will remain constantly with you. The world does not recognize the Spirit of truth, because it does not know the Spirit and is unable to receive Him. But you do know the Spirit because He lives with you, and He will dwell in you.

Being led by the Holy Spirit is a gift, but many choose not to receive the gift, and many have yet to understand the need for this gift in their lives. The Holy Spirit brings you comfort, teaches you truth, and allows you to have close communion with the Lord. However, it's up to you to value this gift. Think of a toddler who has received a gift from his or her parents. The parents are so excited about buying the best gift ever for their toddler. But the toddler opens the gift and spends more time playing with the box and paper that the gift was wrapped in. Leader, value the gift God has given you. In leadership, there will be many, many, many troubles. No one is exempt from troubles, so when trouble comes into your life, allow the Holy Spirit to bring you the comfort you need. Allow the written Word of God to lead you to the truth of a constant God who is with you every day. He cares, and He's aware of everything that concerns you. Gladly welcome and enjoy the gift of the Holy Spirit in your life.

WEEK 21:

John 7:37-39 (MSG) — On the final and climactic day of the Feast, Jesus took his stand. He cried out, "If anyone thirsts, let him come to me and drink. Rivers of living water will brim and spill out of the depths of anyone who believes in me this way, just as the Scripture says." (He said this in regard to the Spirit, whom those who believed in him were about to receive. The Spirit had not yet been given because Jesus had not yet been glorified.)

The Lord never gives us a sense that we need perfection before we can be used for His glory. The scripture says, "If anyone thirsts, let him come to me and drink" — meaning, if anyone needs to be refreshed or replenished, find more than enough in Me. In fact, the Lord is powerful enough to cause this refreshing to flow from you like living water so that He can bless others through your life. Leader, that's exactly where you want to live. Apart from the Lord, your leadership abilities are just human-powered abilities. But when you choose the Lord as your source of knowledge, your source of life, your source of hope, and your source of everything you could ever need, He will cause you to lead on higher heights. The Lord is always more than enough to meet your needs and the needs of those you lead. Let's not fall into the trap of thinking you have gotten good enough to reach people through your own gifts. It is the Lord who saves and strengthens you and calls you according to His purpose for your life. Stay aware of the grace which covers you. You need the Holy Spirit to supply you with grace and comfort in abundance. He is enough to cover you and more than enough to bless others through the way you lead.

WEEK 22:

Zechariah 9:9-10 (The Voice) — Cry out with joy, O daughter of Zion! Shout jubilantly, O daughter of Jerusalem! Look— your King is coming; He is righteous and able to save. He comes seated humbly on a donkey, on a colt, a foal of a donkey. I will dismantle Ephraim's chariots, retire the warhorses from Jerusalem, send home the archers to their families in peace. He will make peace with the nations; His sovereignty will extend from coast to coast, from the Euphrates River to the limits of the earth.

Leader, have you thought about this — Jesus knew the events He was about to face when He had his triumphant entry into Jerusalem. He knew He was going to surrender to death on a cross. He loved the world enough to follow through, fulfill the prophesy, and make a way for everyone to receive a Savior. Knowing the Lord as Savior is the most important relationship you could ever develop. Having the knowledge of how much He loved you before you were even in the position to choose Him as Savior should stir you into action. That action should be making sure everyone around you can see the fruit of the Spirit in you. Love, joy, peace, patience, kindness, goodness, faithfulness, gentleness, and self-control should be evident in your personality. Leader, Jesus gave you an expensive gift that you could never earn — even if you truly tried to pay for it, you couldn't afford the price He paid. Your only response should be to share this precious gift with others.

WEEK 23:

Matthew 20:17-19 (The Voice) — As Jesus was making His way to Jerusalem, He took His twelve disciples aside and once again told them what was about to happen.

Jesus: We are going to Jerusalem. The Son of Man will be betrayed to the chief priests and to the teachers of the law. He will be condemned to death, and the priests and teachers will turn Him over to the Romans, who will mock Him and flog Him and crucify Him. But on the third day, He will be raised from the dead to new resurrected life.

Believers in Jesus Christ are saved because of Jesus's sacrifice for us. But Leader, it's the hope of a full life that resonates the most. It's difficult to fully imagine the pain Jesus endured and the suffering He submitted Himself to, but it's a blessing He thought of the entire world. He endured so everyone can live life knowing He understands our struggles and pain. Even though the issues you face in your role of leadership are great, of course, your struggles and pain seem trivial when compared to the physical anguish and verbal abuse Jesus endured. But you can find strength to live your life, endure pain, triumph over struggles, and glorify God with your life because of Jesus's example. If you are currently overwhelmed by life and facing grave circumstances, know how much God cares for you. Know He loves you no matter what and His love never ends. He has promised to work through the circumstances of life and bring you to a place of joy.

WEEK 24:

Romans 10:10-13 (The Voice) — Belief begins in the heart and leads to a life that's right with God; confession departs from our lips and brings eternal salvation. Because what Isaiah said was true: "The one who trusts in Him will not be disgraced." Remember that the Lord draws no distinction between Jew and non-Jew—He is Lord over all things, and He pours out His treasures on all who invoke His name because as Scripture says, "Everyone who calls on the name of the Lord will be saved."

Faith is not something we do. It is a response to what God has done already on our behalf, the response of a spirit restless in a fragmented world.

What would it look like for you to trust in the Lord? Maybe you need to make yourself rest and get sleep at night. Or you may need to exercise your Christian values in your place of business. You may need to be present in the moment instead of constantly thinking about work. Or you may need to trust that God is leading you and you have everything you need because you trust your source. Whatever you need to do, work on demonstrating your faith in the Lord this week. He has a place for you in heaven when this life is over, but before you get to heaven, you should spend your time living with true joy. Yes, even when things aren't going your way, God is still Lord. You can have joy beyond your own understanding because you believe in the Lord and you actually speak your belief in Jesus Christ. You are saved eternally. You never have to doubt your faith. But, humans tend to doubt and question. It's human nature. That's why you should read the Bible every day. Leader, you are saved, and your Savior makes good on all His promises to you.

WEEK 25:

1 Peter 2:9-10 (The Voice) — But you are a chosen people, set aside to be a royal order of priests, a holy nation, God's own; so that you may proclaim the wondrous acts of the One who called you out of inky darkness into shimmering light. Once you were not a people, but now you are God's people; once you had not received mercy, but now you have received it.

Why live knowing God has chosen you? — because it changes the way you approach your life. You are hand-picked by the Eternal God. The Lord loves you. You are His choice. Think about that for a minute. This means you have what you need to handle your issues and problems. Yes, even when you feel overwhelmed, you're still equipped, even if you are currently facing the unthinkable. The Almighty is with you in the details of your life. It is extremely important for you to rehearse who God is to you. Think about His loving character. He has never failed and never will. Tell Him how worthy He is. He will lead you into the answers for your life. Listening to Him or seeking direction from Him is very important for leaders. He is the source of life. It's fitting for the people He has chosen to want to thank and praise Him. The word "fitting" means it looks and feels good for you. Leader, worship looks good on you!

WEEK 26:

Psalm 95:1-2, 6-7 (The Voice) — Come, let us worship in song, a joyful offering to the Eternal. Shout! Shout with joy to the rock of our liberation. Come face-to-face with God, and give thanks; with loud and joyful voices, praise Him in songs. Come, let us worship Him. Everyone bow down; kneel before the Eternal who made us. For He is our God and we are His people, the flock of His pasture, His sheep protected and nurtured by His hand. Today, if He speaks, hear His voice.

What do you do when you're tired or you've had an extremely long week? Psalm 95 gives you a great answer — you begin with thankfulness, and the rest will follow. If you were to sit and make a list of things you are grateful for, you would see God in all the areas of your life. After you accepted Him as Lord, He took His rightful place as Shepherd of your life, and He takes great care of you. Hear His voice through Scripture, through wise counsel, and through the leading of the Holy Spirit. Then, commit to being thankful, joyful, and excited about the work He's called you to do. That's the way to the heart of God. That's an example of a leader who has been saved by a great and good God.

WEEK 27:

1 Peter 1:6-7 (The Voice) — You should greatly rejoice in what is waiting for you, even if now for a little while you have to suffer various trials. Suffering tests your faith which is more valuable than gold (remember that gold, although it is perishable, is tested by fire) so that if it is found genuine, you can receive praise, honor, and glory when Jesus the Anointed, our Liberating King, is revealed at last.

Early Christians stand apart from the culture and suffer social stigmas and physical persecution at times. Peter challenges them to remain faithful to Jesus who also suffered for not conforming.

Current culture doesn't necessarily hold a disciplined life in high esteem. It's not popular to attend church, be a part of a small group, or live Christian values. But that's precisely why you should accept the calling to serve people. Be different from the culture and set the standard. Nothing on earth can eternally satisfy like a relationship with Jesus. Connecting to the One who made you, knows you, and knows who He created you to be is eternally satisfying. Leader, avoid getting into a toxic cycle of worry. Worry breaks your body down and negatively affects your health. But worship and prayer lift the weight of life off of your heart and place your focus where it should remain — on your Savior. The Lord loves you perfectly and is always waiting for you to spend time putting your cares on Him.

WEEK 28:

Psalm 139:1-6 (The Voice) — O Eternal One, You have explored my heart and know exactly who I am; You even know the small details like when I take a seat and when I stand up again. Even when I am far away, You know what I'm thinking. You observe my wanderings and my sleeping, my waking and my dreaming, and You know everything I do in more detail than even I know. You know what I'm going to say long before I say it. It is true, Eternal One, that You know everything and everyone. You have surrounded me on every side, behind me and before me, and You have placed Your hand gently on my shoulder. It is the most amazing feeling to know how deeply You know me, inside and out; the realization of it is so great that I cannot comprehend it.

It is good to meditate on the omniscience of God and enjoy the comfort of knowing He's got you. That thought alone should light a fire under you to be the best! Yes, be the best leader you can be but also be the best human being you can be. God has perfect knowledge of you, your thoughts, and your motives, and He chooses to love you. He chooses to protect and move you into a deeper understanding of Him. His heart is for and toward His children. He has put you in a great position to serve His people, as well as love them.

WEEK 29:

*Romans 12:5-9 (The Voice) — we, too—the many—
are different parts that form one body in the Anointed
One. Each one of us is joined with one another, and
we become together what we could not be alone.
Since our gifts vary depending on the grace poured
out on each of us, it is important that we exercise
the gifts we have been given. If prophecy is your
gift, then speak as a prophet according to your pro-
portion of faith. If service is your gift, then serve
well. If teaching is your gift, then teach well. If you
have been given a voice of encouragement, then
use it often. If giving is your gift, then be generous.
If leading, then be eager to get started. If sharing
God's mercy, then be cheerful in sharing it. Love
others well, and don't hide behind a mask; love
authentically. Despise evil; pursue what is good as
if your life depends on it.*

Leader, here you find in Scripture the definition of a team.
Teams should function, according to Scripture, as a unit.
God has lovingly given all His children gifts and talents, which
we use in conjunction toward a common goal. This is the way to
being happy carrying out your daily tasks. When you function
in your natural God-given role, it makes room for everyone on
your team to function in their natural God-given roles. As the
leader, you should know everyone's gifts and graces. You are in
a position to make sure everyone is in the best position for their
skill set. How much time have you spent learning everyone's
strengths and weaknesses? When a team has great innovative

leadership and each member of the team knows he or she is a valuable member, it's a sight to behold. Knowing who God created you to be will free you to literally allow love to flow from your heart. Love should be unforced, very calm, and freely given to everyone who needs it. Leader, remember to put all of your confidence in the Holy Spirit to guide you into the person you need to be so that you can truly be effective daily.

WEEK 30:

1 Peter 2:1-7 (The Voice) — So get rid of hatefulness and deception, of insincerity and jealousy and slander. Be like newborn babies, crying out for spiritual milk that will help you grow into salvation if you have tasted and found the Lord to be good. Come to Him—the living stone—who was rejected by people but accepted by God as chosen and precious. Like living stones, let yourselves be assembled into a spiritual house, a holy order of priests who offer up spiritual sacrifices that will be acceptable to God through Jesus the Anointed. For it says in the words of the prophet Isaiah, See here—I am laying in Zion a stone, a cornerstone, chosen and precious; Whoever depends upon Him will never be disgraced. To you who believe and depend on Him, He is precious; but to you who don't, remember the words of the psalmist: The stone that the builders rejected has been laid as the cornerstone—the very stone that holds together the entire foundation,

Allow 1 Peter 2 to give a good reminder of how to treat employees and coworkers. We should always be mindful of how we speak to others, as well as what we say about each other. Never allow jealousy, anger, different viewpoints, or any other damaging, negative things to drive a wedge between members of your team. Speak openly and honestly to each other every day. Leader, you are never above being a disciplined follower of Jesus Christ. Pray, worship, and be in the Lord's presence as you build up your soul. 1 Peter 2: 2 says to desire the Word of God like a baby desires milk. *(Voice Bible, 2.2)* Have you ever been around a screaming, hungry baby who will not shut up until he or she is fed? That's how you have to remain — hungry for the Word of the Lord. Build your life on the foundation of Jesus Christ; He will keep your life together and cover you with grace.

WEEK 31:

Hebrews 12:25-29 (The Voice) — See that you don't turn away from the One who is speaking; for if the ones who heard and refused the One who spoke on earth faced punishment, then how much more will we suffer if we turn away from the One speaking from heaven— the One whose voice in earlier times shook the earth now makes another promise: "Yet once more I will shake not only the earth, but also the heavens"? The phrase, "Yet once more," means that those things that can be shaken will be removed and taken away, namely, the first creation. As a result, those things that remain cannot be shaken. Therefore, let us all be thankful that we are a part of an unshakable Kingdom and offer to God worship that pleases Him and reflects the awe and reverence we have toward Him, for He is like a fierce fire that consumes everything.

Hebrews 12 reminds leaders to remember to include worship, prayer, and hearing from the Lord as a vital part of your weekly preparation. There is no perfect leader, person, or employee — everyone needs the Lord's presence. Get into the habit of consistently remaining in a loop of changing your heart, mind, and, ultimately, how you live because of God's grace shining on your life. You cannot afford to lead without the power of the Holy Spirit. The Holy Spirit will always speak to and correct your heart first so you can be powerful in the workplace. Leader, keep your eyes on the Lord, and He will cause you to be successful.

WEEK 32:

Habakkuk 2:1-3 (The Voice) — I will take my place at the watchtower. I will stand at my post and watch. I will watch and see what He says to me. I need to think about how I should respond to Him When He gets back to me with His answer. Eternal One (to Habakkuk): Write down this vision. Write it clearly on tablets, so that anyone who reads it may run. For the vision points ahead to a time I have appointed; it testifies regarding the end, and it will not lie. Even if there is a delay, wait for it. It is coming and will come without delay.

Leader, what is your guarantee that you are accomplishing the will of the Lord? When you are preparing, you have to be meticulous in your preparation. You must pray and listen to what the Lord has to speak to you. Working hard and getting things set up in just the correct way are all important, but without hearing from the Lord, we won't be able to effectively lead His people long term. The Lord may correct us, caution us, comfort us, or lead us, and we must resolve to submit to Him in His leading. He's always speaking to us so He can speak through us. Leader, write down a plan and follow it because after a time of prayer and listening, you will be ready to make the plan clear and carry out His vision. And you can carry out His vision comfortably because you are staying close to Him. The guarantee is always found in the Lord. Every week, you write the vision, carry out His plans, and depend on Him to move you in the right direction to accomplish His will.

WEEK 33:

Matthew 20:25-28 (The Voice) — Jesus: Do you want the Kingdom run like the Romans run their kingdom? Their rulers have great power over the people, but God the Father doesn't play by the Romans' rules. This is the Kingdom's logic: whoever wants to become great must first make himself a servant; whoever wants to be first must bind himself as a slave— just as the Son of Man did not come to be served, but to serve and to give His life as the ransom for many.

Today's culture is currently set up contrary to this spiritual principle, but this is a principle you should live by. Ask the Lord to search your heart to make sure you represent Him well in this area. Leaders must keep the Lord's example constantly on their minds. Philippians 2: 7-8 says the Lord "poured Himself out *to fill a vessel brand new;* a servant in form and a man indeed. The very likeness of humanity, He humbled Himself, obedient to death— a merciless death on the cross!" *(Voice Bible, 2. 7-8).* If you want to be an effective leader, you have to become a servant. Share your time, your talents, your heart, and Christ's love with an attitude of servanthood. Pray for the Lord to use all He has given you to bless those you lead.

WEEK 34:

From 1 Samuel 16: 7 (NIV) — "Do not consider his appearance or his height, for I have rejected him. The Lord does not look at the things people look at. People look at the outward appearance, but the Lord looks at the heart."

Leader, this scripture is a direct description of the calling God has given us. I am thankful God does not look for an outward show but He looks at your heart. He knows your innermost thoughts and your innermost motivations. As you lead your team, lead them by example. Show them how to have a great attitude daily, how to be an honest person, and how to work hard for the good of the entire team. Make it your desire to grow the individuals on your team. Give them great advice on how to move to the next level in the company. Really make it your priority for each team member to reach his or her goals within the company. Do this as you thank the Lord for the mentors who helped you get to where you are today. The Lord is forever good and gracious to you. Share His goodness with others as much as you possibly can.

WEEK 35:

Philippians 3:9-14 (The Voice) — When it counts, I want to be found belonging to Him, not clinging to my own righteousness based on law, but actively relying on the faithfulness of the Anointed One. This is true righteousness, supplied by God, acquired by faith. I want to know Him inside and out. I want to experience the power of His resurrection and join in His suffering, shaped by His death, so that I may arrive safely at the resurrection from the dead.

The crucified and risen Jesus is the model that Paul desires to embody by walking deep in His pathway of death and life—suffering and resurrection.

I'm not there yet, nor have I become perfect; but I am charging on to gain anything and everything the Anointed One, Jesus, has in store for me—and nothing will stand in my way because He has grabbed me and won't let me go. Brothers and sisters, as I said, I know I have not arrived; but there's one thing I am doing: I'm leaving my old life behind, putting everything on the line for this mission. I am sprinting toward the only goal that counts: to cross the line, to win the prize, and to hear God's call to resurrection life found exclusively in Jesus the Anointed.

It is human nature to want to have an easy life free of problems — especially problems you didn't create yourself. Poor judgment is the source of some problems, but sometimes, unpleasant situations are lurking around the corner, and that's just the way life is sometimes. Leaders who are true followers of Jesus can many times attract problems because of spiritual warfare. There are spiritual forces in this world who are against you trying something new or you getting a revelation from the Lord. These forces are against you growing because it would build up the kingdom of God. These forces also know great leaders serve, as well as care for the people they lead. Philippians 3 is a great reminder for you to be on guard from allowing trouble to stop you from being the best leader possible. Leave the past behind and pick up the tools God has placed in your hand. These tools are love, joy, peace, patience, kindness, goodness, faithfulness, gentleness, and self-control. These are the fruit of the Holy Spirit. Leader, you have more than enough of this fruit in your life and heart to lead effectively.

WEEK 36:

Matthew 5:1-3 (The Voice) — People talk about this Jesus, this Preacher and Healer. Word spreads of His charisma and wisdom and power and love. People who are too sick to walk persuade their friends and relatives to carry them to Jesus. These cripples and demonized and ill and paralytics come to Jesus, and He heals them, and they follow Him. Now when He saw the crowds, He went up on a mountain (as Moses had done before Him) and He sat down (as Jewish teachers of His day usually did). His disciples gathered around Him. There on the mountain Jesus teaches them all. And as He is teaching, crowds gather around and overhear His teachings, listen in, and are captivated. This, the Sermon on the Mount, is the first of the five Mosaic-like sermons in Matthew. And He began to teach them. Jesus: Blessed are the spiritually poor—the kingdom of heaven is theirs.

This passage describes Jesus as the leader of all leaders! "News of Jesus' charisma, wisdom, power, and love spread throughout the land." *(Voice Bible, 5.1-12)* This news compelled crowds of people to come to listen to Jesus teach. Leader, pray for that same spirit to grow in you. Work toward leading with charisma, wisdom, power, and love. As a leader, your personality should be attractive. People should enjoy your leadership abilities. You can accomplish this by having the attitude of seeking God's will to be done for you and for the people you are leading. Remain humble and lead by setting an example of one who follows the teachings of the Lord.

WEEK 37:

Isaiah 41:8-10 (The Voice) — Eternal One: But you, My servant, Israel, Jacob whom I have chosen and descendant of My friend, Abraham, I have reached to wherever you are in the farthest corners of earth, and the most hidden places therein. I have called to you and said, "You are my servant. I have chosen you, not thrown you away!" So don't be afraid. I am here, with you; don't be dismayed, for I am your God. I will strengthen you, help you. I am here with My right hand to make right and to hold you up.

Leader, think about the promises God has spoken to you in the past. If you cannot think of any promises, here are three promises of many found in Scripture you'll want to remember. The Lord promises to be with you daily, He promises to love you without condition, and He promises to give you supernatural strength. For sure, God has called you into leadership. You are successful in fulfilling your calling because of Him. As you spend time in prayer, pray about the promises you find in Scripture, as well as the promises the Lord has given you personally. As you pray, focus on believing in faith that the Lord will be faithful to you. He is your God. Face your week believing in the strength He's promised to give you.

WEEK 38:

Psalm 133:1-3 (The Voice) — A song of David for those journeying to worship.

How good and pleasant it is when brothers and sisters live together in peace! It is like the finest oils poured on the head, sweet-smelling oils flowing down to cover the beard, Flowing down the beard of Aaron, flowing down the collar of his robe. It is like the gentle rain of Mount Hermon that falls on the hills of Zion. Yes, from this place, the Eternal spoke the command, from there He gave His blessing — life forever.

The opportunity to work with people and their various personalities is a blessing some leaders tend to overlook. Have you fallen into a routine of forgetting to be grateful for the people God has called you to lead? How about praying for everyone you lead — are you praying for them? The Lord has the gracious ability to strategically place you among people who challenge, inspire, sometimes frustrate, and push you to grow! Leader, you need the people you are leading, and they need you. You are in the middle of a blessed life. May God be glorified through the way you lead and work with people in unity and peace.

WEEK 39:

Psalm 27:4-7 (The Voice) — I am pleading with the Eternal for this one thing, my soul's desire: To live with Him all of my days—in the shadow of His temple, To behold His beauty and ponder His ways in the company of His people. His house is my shelter and secret retreat. It is there I find peace in the midst of storm and turmoil. Safety sits with me in the hiding place of God. He will set me on a rock, high above the fray God lifts me high above those with thoughts of death and deceit that call for my life. I will enter His presence, offering sacrifices and praise. In His house, I am overcome with joy. As I sing, yes, and play music for the Eternal alone. I cannot shout any louder. Eternal One—hear my cry and respond with Your grace.

Each psalm is poetry set to music. Psalm 27 reminds you to abide with the Lord. Our days can sometimes be filled with different levels of troubles, but Leader, even when your day isn't smooth and serene, don't allow your ego to trick you into thinking you don't need time with the Lord. When problems come up, it's easy to go into a hyper mode of fixing people or micromanaging people. Your team needs to have the room to problem solve. Be the calming presence because you've given yourself enough time to start each day being thankful, reading Scripture, worshiping, praying, or simply sitting still in the Lord's presence. Leader, your calling to be in leadership was never meant to negate your need for personal time with your Father. You will never have the spiritual insight needed to lead the best you can without spending personal time adoring the Lord. Take some time this week to read the entire chapter of Psalm 27 and see how the Lord is speaking to you through His Holy Word.

WEEK 40:

Romans 15:1-7 (The Voice) — So now what? We who are strong are not just to satisfy our own desires. We are called to carry the weaknesses of those who are not strong. Each of us must strive to please our neighbors, pursuing their welfare so they will become strong. The Anointed One Himself is our model for this kind of living, for He did not live to please Himself. And as the Scriptures declared, "When they insult You, they insult me." You see, everything written in the days of old was recorded to give us instructions for living. We find encouragement through the Scriptures and a call to perseverance that will produce hopeful living. I pray that our God, who calls you and gives you perseverance and encouragement, will join all of you together to share one mind according to Jesus the Anointed. In this unity, you will share one voice as you glorify the one True God, the Father of our Lord Jesus, the Anointed One, our Liberating King. So accept one another in the same way the Anointed has accepted you so that God will get the praise He is due.

Leader, when you read the entire chapter of Romans 15, you learn Paul is bringing out the concept of laying down personal objectives or personal preferences for the good of the community we live in. Just as Jesus sacrificed, you are His example to the world. There are certain things you should sacrifice and instead seek justice, peace, kindness, and love for all. Being in a leadership role requires spiritual strength. You are engaging others to work in unison and leading them to humble their individual attitudes while working for the good of the whole. Without submission, a team cannot operate as a community working to achieve a goal. Your team's determination to achieve the overall goal trumps other personal goals. This is a huge task that requires preparation. Take ample time before each day to meditate on Scripture and lead with joy. When there is no joy in serving in a community, it corrodes the blessing of having the opportunity to serve.

WEEK 41:

1 Chronicles 16:28-34 (The Voice) — Give all credit to the Eternal, families of the world! Credit Him with honor and strength! Credit Him with the glory worthy of His magnificent name; gather your sacrifice, and present it before Him. Bow down to the Eternal, adorned in holiness. Fear Him, all the earth. For the earth is firmly rooted; it cannot move. Heavens, be glad; earth, rejoice. Say to the nations, "The Eternal One reigns." The sea roars, as do its creatures. The field rejoices, as do its crops. Then will the forest and its trees cry out before the Eternal, for He comes to judge the earth. Give testimony about the Eternal because He is good; His loyal love lasts forever.

When you have time, go back and read all of 1 Chronicles 16. It is a great scripture for your personal meditation time. Personal time with the Lord is so important for every leader, but with meetings and schedules, it is so difficult to keep this time sacred. Never get down on yourself when you go a while without personal time with the Lord. God isn't judging you, but when you find yourself going extended times without time with the Lord, make some adjustments in your schedule to get back on track. Leader, you really need your time with Him. You can't lead people where you haven't been or where you haven't been lately. Use scripture like 1 Chronicles 16 as a guide. Pray this scripture as worship to the Lord. It's appropriate to whisper worship and thanks to the Lord first thing in the morning, during the day while leading with excellence, and at the end of the day before you drift off to sleep in peace. This is how God designed you to live — praying without ceasing and glorifying Him all day.

WEEK 42:

John 15: 9-17 (The Voice) — At a time when all of His disciples are feeling as if they are about to be uprooted, Jesus sketches a picture of this new life as a flourishing vineyard—a labyrinth of vines and strong branches steeped in rich soil, abundant grapes hanging from their vines ripening in the sun. Jesus sculpts a new garden of Eden in their imaginations—one that is bustling with fruit, sustenance, and satisfying aromas. This is the Kingdom life. It is all about connection, sustenance, and beauty. But within this promise of life is the warning that people must be in Christ or they will not experience these blessings.

Jesus: I have loved you as the Father has loved Me. Abide in My love. Follow My example in obeying the Father's commandments and receiving His love. If you obey My commandments, you will stay in My love. I want you to know the delight I experience, to find ultimate satisfaction, which is why I am telling you all of this. My commandment to you is this: love others as I have loved you. There is no greater way to love than to give your life for your friends. You celebrate our friendship if you obey this command. I don't call you servants any longer; servants don't know what the master is doing, but I have told you everything the Father has said to Me. I call you friends. You did not choose Me. I chose you, and I orchestrated all of this so that you would be sent out and bear great and perpetual fruit. As you do this, anything you ask the Father in My name will be done. This is My command to you: love one another.

Even leaders sometimes still struggle with the big questions in life — am I called and what am I called to? John 15 is a great reminder to love people. If you are busy loving others, you're within the calling God has placed on your life. This scripture passage is a reminder to avoid getting caught up in whether you're in the right place every moment of your life. Instead, focus on making sure people are confirmed in following your leadership. Fixating on the worst in people is the opposite of loving them. If you take it a step further, fixating on the worst in people will only allow you to experience the worst when you're with them. Lead people with the idea in mind to share your life with them and love them.

WEEK 43:

Luke 9:46-48 (NIV) — An argument started among the disciples as to which of them would be the greatest. Jesus, knowing their thoughts, took a little child and had him stand beside him. Then he said to them, "Whoever welcomes this little child in my name welcomes me; and whoever welcomes me welcomes the one who sent me. For it is the one who is least among you all who is the greatest."

Leader, you have a relationship with the Lord. Know He is always near to you. But have you spent time lately thinking of how the Lord knows you intimately? He is aware of your thoughts, your motivations, and your actions. Normally, you would take comfort knowing the Lord is aware of you when you are hurting, but He is also aware of the condition of your heart even when you aren't hurting. He concerns Himself with His children all the time. If you have the spirit of comparison or the spirit of trying to one up another leader for any reason, ask the Lord to change that spirit in you. You should maintain the spirit of humble leadership and making sure you are doing everything to help your team be successful. You want the Lord to work through your efforts and find you faithful in not comparing yourself to others in hopes of edging the competition out. All of your focus remains on Jesus Christ. He placed you where you are for a reason, and He will allow you to stay there until the times comes for you to move to the next leadership position.

WEEK 44:

Psalm 50:14-23 (The Voice) — Set out a sacrifice I can accept: your thankfulness. Be true to your word to the Most High. When you are in trouble, call for Me. I will come and rescue you, and you will honor Me." But to those acting against Him, God says, "Who do you think you are? Listing off My laws, acting as if your life is in alignment with My ways? For it's clear that you despise My guidance; you throw My wise words over your shoulder. You play with thieves, spend your time with adulterers. Evil runs out of your mouth; your tongue is wrapped in deceit. You sit back and gossip about your brother; you slander your mother's son. While you did these things, I kept silent; somehow you got the idea that I was like you. But now My silence ends, and I am going to indict you. I'll state the charge against you clearly, face-to-face. All you who have forgotten Me, your God, should think about what I have said, or I will tear you apart and leave no one to save you. Set out a sacrifice I can accept: your thankfulness. Do this, and you will honor Me. Those who straighten up their lives will know the saving grace of God."

Leader, how do you abide in Christ? Do you ever put aside your long list of things to accomplish to connect with the Lord in some way while at work? Sometimes, it's just what the doctor ordered. Psalm 50 can serve as your reminder to keep from obeying the law and thinking you have everything down. Leaders must live in a cycle of confession, thanksgiving, and giving the Lord glory. If you neglect to acknowledge the Lord in private, you cannot expect His Spirit to work through you in public. You really need His direction, guidance, presence, love, joy, peace, etc. on a daily basis. Think of the chorus from the hymn, "I Need Thee Every Hour" by Anne Franke:

I need Thee, oh, I need Thee; Every hour I need Thee;
Oh, bless me now, my Savior! I come to Thee.

Hawks, A. (1872). I need thee every hour [Lyrics]. Retrieved from https://hymnary.org/ text/i_need_thee_every_hour_most_gracious_lor

WEEK 45:

Ephesians 2: 17-22 (The Voice) — The Great Preacher of peace and love came for you, and His voice found those of you who were near and those who were far away. By Him both have access to the Father in one Spirit. And so you are no longer called outcasts and wanderers but citizens with God's people, members of God's holy family, and residents of His household. You are being built on a solid foundation: the message of the prophets and the voices of God's chosen emissaries with Jesus, the Anointed Himself, the precious cornerstone. The building is joined together stone by stone—all of us chosen and sealed in Him, rising up to become a holy temple in the Lord. In Him you are being built together, creating a sacred dwelling place among you where God can live in the Spirit.

Leader, do you think of God as the God of love? Ephesians 2 describes the Lord as the God of peace and love. These are the two things every leader needs more of. You can have as much peace and love as you need to lead because God is peace and love. His Spirit lives in you. You live in the presence of God because of Jesus. You have the opportunity to worship, to serve, to lead, and to have a more meaningful relationship with God because of Jesus's sacrifice. Consider this — how can you access the God of peace and love to make an effort to be more engaging in your work? Here are some practical things — 1) believe the Holy Spirit is at work in you and allow Him to lead you into great ideas to creatively lead. 2) Prepare yourself mentally before entering your place of business by thanking the Lord for your peace and love. 3) Stay mindful of your thoughts and your emotions while at work. Make sure you are always leading from a place of peace and love. If you run into a situation that causes you to become emotional, take a minute to examine your emotions and settle them before proceeding. Leader, you can become closer to Christ even as you function in your role as a leader if you will stay aware of the Holy Spirit within you.

Philippians 1:3-11 (The Voice) — Whenever you cross my mind, I thank my God for you and for the gift of knowing you. My spirit is lightened with joy whenever I pray for you (and I do constantly) because you have partnered with me to spread the gospel since the first day I preached to you. I am confident that the Creator, who has begun such a great work among you, will not stop in mid-design but will keep perfecting you until the day Jesus the Anointed, our Liberating King, returns to redeem the world. It is only right that I should feel such admiration for you all—you hold me close to your hearts. And, since we are partners in this great work of grace, you have never failed to stand with me as I have defended and stood firm for the gospel—even from this prison cell. Before God I want you to know how much I long to see you and love you with the affection of the Anointed One, Jesus. Here's what I pray for you: Father, may their love grow more and more in wisdom and insight— so they will be able to examine and determine the best from everything else. And on the day of the Anointed One, the day of His judgment, let them stand pure and blameless, filled with the fruit of righteousness that ripens through Jesus the Anointed.

The apostle Paul wrote this letter to the saints in Philippi. This scripture is often read around Thanksgiving because it can lead you to be thankful for the community of believers

God has placed you in. So many times, leaders put way too much attention on the small things that aren't working out in their lives as they'd hoped and spend too little time actually being thankful for their faith community or church community. Being overly critical, bogged down with worry, or mentally rehearsing negativity is a trap keeping you from having true joy. Also, remember to be transparent in sharing real things in your life with your church small group. It increases your joy when you have a group of people who expect you to attend church weekly and who pray with you over the details of your life. Leaders who share their lives and Christian walks with others tend to be settled within themselves, peaceful, and happy.

WEEK 47:

Colossians 2:6-7 (The Voice) — Now that you have welcomed the Anointed One, Jesus the Lord, into your lives, continue to journey with Him and allow Him to shape your lives. Let your roots grow down deeply in Him, and let Him build you up on a firm foundation. Be strong in the faith, just as you were taught, and always spill over with thankfulness.

Thankfulness is a choice. Take a minute to reflect on things, people, family members, and coworkers you are thankful for. Your hope, your future, and your direction always come from the Lord, who is at work within you to lead others well. There are so many people living every day without the knowledge of Jesus Christ and without the knowledge of their purpose in life. Leader, you may not have every single detail of your life figured out, but you do know how to walk with the Lord and trust Him for guidance. He is shaping your life, and He's working through you as a leader to help shape other people's lives. Continue in the important work of being thankful every day.

WEEK 48:

Romans 1:5-12 (The Voice) — And here's what He's done: He has graced us and sanctioned us as His emissaries whose mission is to spread the one true and obedient faith to all people in the name of Jesus. This includes you: you have been called by Jesus, God's Anointed. To all those who are God's beloved saints in Rome: May grace and peace from God our Father and the Lord Jesus, the Anointed One, surround you. First, I thank my God through Jesus the Anointed for all of you because we are joined by faith as family, and your faith is spreading across the world. For I call God as my witness—whom I worship in my spirit and serve in making known the gospel—He alone knows how often I mention you in my prayers. I find myself constantly praying for you and hoping it's in God's will for me to be with you soon. I desperately want to see you so that I can share some gift of the Spirit to strengthen you. Plus I know that when we come together something beautiful will happen as we are encouraged by each other's faith.

You don't get to choose the people you work with. Sometimes, there's great chemistry among employees, and other times, huge issues arise. As the leader of your group, what can you do to model relationship building and teamwork? When people are known, really known, they tend to enjoy the work they do and remain an employee for years. Leader, give people the gift of "belonging." Create a work environment where people can share details of their lives in a trusting environment. Stay away from making jokes at employees' expense, especially when that person isn't present. Instead, speak about positive things by rehearsing the things God is teaching you and how you are becoming more like Him. Romans 1:12 states it beautifully, "I know that when we come together something beautiful will happen as we are encouraged by each other's faith." Leader, you can make small tweaks to create a better work environment where people have the sense of "belonging."

WEEK 49:

Psalm 28:7-9 (The Voice) — The Eternal is the source of my strength and the shield that guards me. When I learn to rest and truly trust Him, He sends His help. This is why my heart is singing! I open my mouth to praise Him, and thankfulness rises as song. The Eternal gives life and power to all His chosen ones; to His anointed He is a sturdy fortress. Rescue Your people, and bring prosperity to Your legacy; may they know You as a shepherd, carrying them at all times.

Leader, it's important for you to remember some of the simple things about your relationship with the Lord. Sometimes, we have to bring things to our conscious memory, or we will forget. The Lord is your hope, your shield, your peace, and your strength. If you don't remember to look at your past and keep watch over how God has turned your life into something glorious, you could find yourself in a situation where your faith has weakened. Through bad choices, sicknesses, weaknesses, and through all kinds of ups and downs, the Lord has chosen you to be a leader. He has brought you to a place where you thrive in glorifying Him. Thank Him every day for being a great Shepherd to you and then turn and be a great leader to those under your leadership.

WEEK 50:

John 14:23-24 (The Voice) — Jesus: Anyone who loves Me will listen to My voice and obey. The Father will love him, and We will draw close to him and make a dwelling place within him. The one who does not love Me ignores My message, which is not from Me, but from the Father who sent Me.

Leader, remember to continue praying for the people you lead. Many times, people won't openly share their issues. You may be leading individuals battling cancer, dealing with the effects of depression, going through issues surrounding a death of a loved one, or trying to wade through divisive issues in their families. Take just ten minutes to worship first then pray for people. Everyone in leadership should take the time to worship. Leader, worship will help you rehearse who God is, and it will honor the Lord. After you've worshiped or honored Him, pray and pray often. This will keep you close to the Lord. You may find that you're less concerned with small issues you're facing when you're focused on praying about the real, serious issues those you are leading are facing.

WEEK 51:

Matthew 9:18-22 (The Voice) — As He was saying these things, a certain official came before Jesus and knelt in front of Him. Official: My daughter just died. Would You come and lay Your hands on her? Then, I know, she would live again. Jesus got up, and He and His disciples went with the man. But as they were heading to the man's house, a woman who had been hemorrhaging and bleeding for 12 years—12 years!—crept up behind Jesus. She evidently believes that if she so much as touches the fringes of His cloak, she will be healed. And so she came up behind Him and touched His cloak. Jesus turned around and saw her. Jesus: Take heart, daughter. Your faith has healed you. And indeed, from that moment, the woman was healed.

Leader, seek the Lord's will for your life every day and remember to always search the condition of your heart. In all your business dealings, remain obedient to the Lord, love others as Christ has loved you, and serve others, believing it is Christ who has appointed you as a leader. Success and failures happen in business every day. It may be tempting to blame failures on others while reserving the glory for all the successes. Read the verses from Matthew 9 again. Humility is a huge theme in these verses. The official in verse 18 had to be a humble person to go to the Lord and kneel before Him. Asking for healing is admitting our current condition is out of our control and the answer to our current condition lies in going to the One who is in control for healing. The woman in this scripture had done everything she could do to be healed of her issue, but it was her faith in Jesus Christ that compelled her to reach out to Jesus for her complete healing. Never forget our desperate need for a Savior. Everything you do is for the glory, honor, and praise of the Lord. Without Him, our lives would fail. He always makes the difference in our lives.

WEEK 52:

Philippians 4:8-9 (The Voice) — Finally, brothers and sisters, fill your minds with beauty and truth. Meditate on whatever is honorable, whatever is right, whatever is pure, whatever is lovely, whatever is good, whatever is virtuous and praiseworthy. Keep to the script: whatever you learned and received and heard and saw in me—do it—and the God of peace will walk with you.

Have you ever noticed how efficient you are when you walk with the Lord faithfully and operate under His peace? When you are peaceful, you can concentrate on serving someone else's needs, but when your own heart is troubled, humans tend to focus inward. Philippians 4 encourages you to meditate, but meditation can be a scary word for leaders. It sounds like sitting still and doing nothing, which is weird and unproductive. However, meditation can simply mean praying a short prayer throughout the day or saying a short scripture to yourself several times a day or even playing a song with a meaning based in Scripture on repeat. Any way of getting the truth of God in your system can be meditation. Leader, staying close to the Lord is the only way to learn who He is so you can show others His grace. The Lord's peace will be with you and remain with you as you stay close to Him while doing what He's appointed you to do.

WEEK 53:

2 King 3: 15-19 (The Voice)–But now, bring me a musician! While the musician was playing, Elisha was empowered by the Eternal. Elisha: This is the Eternal's message: "Dig trenches throughout this entire valley." This is the Eternal's message: "You will not see rain fall from the sky **or feel wind** *blow across your skin,* **but you will see this** *valley filled with water. You and your livestock will have plenty of* **water to quench your thirst!"** *And that's not all!* **It is indeed a small thing for the Eternal One: He is also going to hand the Moabites over to you. Then you will attack every fortified and prosperous city, chop down every decent tree, plug up every water hole, and use stones to destroy every healthy piece of land** *along your way.*

In this scripture, three kings are traveling together, and they need a word from the Lord before they continue on their journey and before they move to defeat the Moabites. They discover they have Elisha, a prophet of the Lord, traveling with them. Elisha is described as someone who carries the message and the power of the Lord with Him. Before Elisha gives the kings a word from the Lord, he asks for a minstrel or a musician to play to set the atmosphere so he can commune with the Lord. As the musician plays, Elisha receives direction from the Lord, and he gives that message to the kings. Then the kings have the assurance to continue their travels, knowing the Lord is with them and will provide for their people. Worship music can be a powerful tool for leaders. When you need answers or direction, download your favorite worship music and allow it to influence your atmosphere. Your wisdom should always come from the Lord. Leader, you need divine direction from the Lord. Consider how worship music can help you praise the Lord and be in His presence. When the Lord is present, His perspective reigns. Remember to lead as the Lord's perspective influences your own perspective.

CONSIDER THE FOLLOWING QUESTIONS:

1) How has your leadership style changed? What evidence do you have to prove your leadership has changed for the better?

2) What have you learned about yourself through the process of searching through Scripture for leadership tips?

3) Write down three changes you've made in your personal life and the result of those changes. Consider how to make these changes permanent as you continue to be a True Leader with Heart.

ABOUT THE AUTHOR

Karla describes herself as a normal mom wearing many hats. She has been married to Dr. Roosevelt Nivens Jr. (a public school superintendent of schools) for nineteen years. Karla and Roosevelt have two teenage children – Naomi and Roosevelt III. The Nivens family resides in Nevada, TX.

After graduating from Texas Tech University, Karla earned her teaching certificate and began her career as an elementary music teacher in the Dallas Independent School District. After staying at home with her children for several years, Karla re-entered the workforce as a worship leader at Highland Park United Methodist Church. Karla has worshipped with Highland Park for the past fifteen years. Karla also served as an adjunct instructor for Visible Music College for several years. She released a CD entitled *True Worship* in 2014, and she hosts her own weekly radio show, "Every Heart Every Woman," which airs Sundays at 6:00 pm CST on 100.7 FM The WORD. It is the joy of Karla's life to volunteer weekly for Love Ministries, a 501(c)(3) non-profit organization founded by Karla's parents in 2005.

Karla Nivens
karlanivens.com
@karlanivensentertainment
ehewradio.com
@ehewradio
karla@karlanivens.com